21 DAYS 4 TEENS

Tiyanah Wilson

Acknowledgements

SOMEBODY PRAYED FOR ME....

Wow! God is so amazing! Talk about Amazing Grace, Thank you God for using a wretch like me . My praying grandmother Mary Edgerton. On those days where my faith was non-exsistent , I know it was your unwavering Faith & consistent prayers that kept me covered. Grandma Debbie , I always wanted to make you proud as your oldest grand and I didn't always feel like I accomplished that. I pray that you're smiling down from heaven knowing that I didn't give up. I miss you so much and this moment is definitely for you. Marcus Wilson, my God ordained King, we are a living testament of Gods work. Thank you for understanding that me tapping in with God is necessary on those days where it cuts into "we time". You have no idea how much your support brings Peace to my life. I Love You baby! Elder Traci Skinner (Mother/Confidant/Best Friend), Tamara Latta, and Tiombe Bassett, my prayer circle. Thank you for consistently refilling me and covering me. If you don't have people that's going to go to spiritual war with you, check your team. Daily , I thank God for y'all.

COREY, ROBBIE, SADE, & RAYDEN, I'LL DO ANYTHING NECESSARY FOR ALL OF YOU. MY FIRST BABIES. THE VERY BEST BROTHERS AND SISTER A GIRL COULD ASK FOR. I WILL CONTINUE TO STRIVE TO BE A GREAT EXAMPLE AND SUPPORT EACH OF YOU IN EVERYTHING YOU DO. NATASHA, THANK YOU FOR SHOWING ME THAT GENUINE HEARTS AND FORGIVENESS STILL EXISTS IN THE WORLD. MY ENTIRE LIFE MISSED YOU ! I'M LIVING PROOF THAT ALL THINGS ARE POSSIBLE TO HIM WHO BELIEVES!

Week 1

Jerimiah 1:5 *NIV*
"Before I formed you in the womb I knew you, before you were born I set you apart; I appointed you as a prophet to the nations."

I wish i knew this scripture before I locked myself in that janitors closet my second week of 6th grade and tried to take my life. Shaking my head now just thinking about how foolish of me it was to want to die because I didn't feel accepted by my peers or like I fit in with any of the crowds. Why would I fit in when GOD set me apart? GOD set US apart! Middle school was just so different. A new school and although there were some familiar faces from elementary school, they were very few. Hart Middle was a huge school in East Orange, NJ that was broken up into 3 buildings. This is where just about everyone who graduated grade school ended up. Imagine trying to find yourself in one school, while having to be in competition with two other schools for being the coolest, most athletic, and having the best academics. Right now looking back, it doesn't seem like a big deal, but when I was going through it , I felt like it was the end of the world. The things that trouble you during this time in your life matter. Your feelings are valid. The frustration, confusion, self doubt, mistakes, self hate, fears, and being misunderstood is all about to make sense in 21 Days.

You were destined for greatness before you were even born. YES YOU! Did you know that God set you apart from the others before you even got here? Take a minute to process that. The creator of the Heavens and the Earth already had a plan set for your life. A plan to prosper you and give you hope and a future. (Jeremiah 29:11) No matter what your past looks like, your future is bright! During this first week, were going to tackle forgiveness, self worth, and self love. These are usually the biggest roadblocks on the road to freedom. Flashback to 4th grade, I was bullied by the tallest girl in the school. I would go home crying to my parents until finally they said " If someone hits you, hit them back?!" Surely, they didn't want me being violent on the school yard, however they didn't want me to continue in life not standing up for myself. That was a great lesson , but what it really taught me was how to be the Queen of revenge during my teenage years. I saw forgiveness as a sign of weakness and I carried an eye for an eye mentality. As you dive into week ones scriptures, you'll learn the importance of forgiveness towards others and most importantly yourself. Buckle Up! It's time for the reroute, restoration, and renewing!

Week 1 Scriptures

Leviticus 19:18 (NIV) - Do not seek revenge or bear a grudge against anyone among your people, but love your neighbor as yourself.

Matthew 6:15 (NIV) - But if you do not forgive others their sins, your Father will not forgive your sins.

John 3:16 (NIV) - For God so loved the world that he gave his one and only Son, that whoever believes in him shall not perish but have eternal life.

Isaiah 50:7 (NIV) - Because the Sovereign Lord helps me, I will not be disgraced. Therefore have I set my face like flint, and I know I will not be put to shame.

Genesis 1:26 (NIV) - Then God said, "Let us make mankind in our image, in our likeness, so that they may rule over the fish in the sea and the birds in the sky, over the livestock and all the wild animals, and over all the creatures that move along the ground.

Psalm 139:14 (ESV) - I praise you, for I am fearfully and wonderfully made. Wonderful are your works; my soul knows it very well.

Jeremiah 29:11 (NIV) - For I know the plans I have for you," declares the Lord, "plans to prosper you and not to harm you, plans to give you hope and a future.

Forgiveness is a blessing blocker if we choose to hold a grudge and be angry with those who hurt us. I'm sure at your age, you've made your fare share of mistakes, and if I can be 100% honest with you, they keep happening even as you become adults. The same forgiveness that you don't want to give, will be the same forgiveness that you need time and time again throughout life. Our first scripture teaches us Gods law on how we have to forgive others and love them like we love ourselves which almost seems impossible until we get to the next scripture. If we don't extend forgiveness, we don't receive forgiveness. I already told you, the mistakes are going to keep happening. I wish I could tell you that once you hit a certain age, life makes sense and you suddenly get it, and never make mistakes again, but that would be a bold face lie. Knowing you're going to make mistakes and need forgiveness should make it a lot easier to extend it. We are imperfect creatures created by a Perfect GOD. You see he knew we would make mistakes and he loves us so much that he sent his only son to die on the cross for our sins. Do you see how special you are? That means that even when we're not our best, God still sees us as his masterpiece. Do you see yourself being made in his image? Do you see yourself as a heir to the greatest kingdom of them all? You were fearfully and wonderfully made. Each and everyone of us, special in our own unique way. From the moment we were in our mother's womb, he had a plan for our lives. Plans to prosper us, give us hope, and a future. Hold on to these truths as you dive into week one journal exercise.

Vibes from Week One

What are some things you would like to release and forgive yourself for?

Write a List of people you choose to forgive.

Which of week one's scriptures stands out to you the most and why?

Does knowing what God says about you change the way you view yourself?

LET'S PRAY

DEAR GOD,

THANK YOU FOR YOUR UNFAILING LOVE FOR ME. I KNOW I'M NOT PERFECT AND I CHOOSE TO SEEK AND RECEIVE YOUR FORGIVENESS DAILY. HELP ME TO RELEASE ANY ANGER, GUILT, OR SHAME THAT I MAY BE CARRYING FROM PAST SITUATIONS SO THAT I CAN EXPERIENCE LIVING IN THE FULLNESS OF YOU. HELP ME TO REMEMBER THAT I WAS CREATED IN YOUR IMAGE AND LIKENESS WHEN I START TO QUESTION MY WORTH OR WONDER IF I'M GOOD ENOUGH. HELP ME TO HAVE A HEART OF COMPASSION SO THAT IT'S NOT HARD FOR ME TO FORGIVE OTHERS JUST LIKE YOU FORGIVE ME. WE ALL HAVE IMPERFECTIONS, BUT YOU ARE A PERFECT GOD LOVING US IN THE MIDST OF THEM. IT MAKES ME EXCITED TO KNOW THAT YOU HAVE A PLAN FOR MY LIFE. TO PROSPER ME AND TO GIVE ME HOPE AND A FUTURE. HELP ME TO CLING TO YOUR WORD WHEN THINGS HAPPEN TO DISTRACT ME FROM THE TRUTH. I'M LOOKING FORWARD TO HAVING A LONG LASTING, STRONG RELATIONSHIP WITH YOU GOD. THANK YOU FOR LEADING AND GUIDING ME ON THIS JOURNEY. IN JESUS NAME,

AMEN

Week 2

Romans 8: 37-39 NIV

No, in all these things we are more than conquerors through him who loved us. For I am convinced that neither death nor life, neither angels nor demons,[b] neither the present nor the future, nor any powers, neither height nor depth, nor anything else in all creation, will be able to separate us from the love of God that is in Christ Jesus our Lord.

When I was younger , I remember going into the kitchen when i felt my parents were preoccupied and I would climb onto the cabinets and pull out the seasonings. Then I would grab some lunch meat or food out the fridge and pretend to be a chef and season that meat to perfection. Although, I ended becoming a professional chef in life, back then all my parents saw was wasted food and wasted money. They would get so upset and I would be put on punishment because I didn't understand value and hard work. Every time I decided to go play in the food in the kitchen and waste it, my parents had to figure out how to replace that so my brothers and I had 3 meals a day plus snacks. While my actions may have frustrated my parents, it didn't change the fact that they love me.

My mistakes didn't separate me from their love and your mistakes can't separate you from Gods love. My parents should actually be happy that they get a little credit when asked when did my career as a chef start HA! HA!
In week two, were going to learn a little bit more about who God is and what he is capable of doing in your life. Having a better understanding of that will help you become more confident in God, and help you become more comfortable going to him with your BOLD PRAYERS!

Week 2 Scriptures

Numbers 23:19 (NIV) - God is not human, that he should lie, not a human being, that he should change his mind. Does he speak and then not act? Does he promise and not fulfill?.

Exodus 14:14 (NIV) - The Lord will fight for you; you need only to be still."

Matthew 6:26 (NIV) - Look at the birds of the air; they do not sow or reap or store away in barns, and yet your heavenly Father feeds them. Are you not much more valuable than they?

Psalm 84:11-12(NIV) - For the Lord God is a sun and shield; the Lord bestows favor and honor; no good thing does he withhold from those whose walk is blameless; Lord Almighty blessed is the one who trusts in you.

1 John 3:1 (NIV) - See what great love the Father has lavished on us, that we should be called children of God! And that is what we are! The reason the world does not know us is that it did not know him.

2 Peter 3:9 (NIV) -The Lord is not slow in keeping his promise, as some understand slowness. Instead he is patient with you, not wanting anyone to perish, but everyone to come to repentance.

Proverbs 19:21 (NIV) - Many are the plans in a person's heart, but it is the Lord's purpose that prevails.

Throughout life , you're going to encounter a lot of different people and they're not always going to have your best interest at heart . Some will make promises and they won't keep their word. Perhaps you've already experienced that already in your life and it hurts. God is not like man. We can trust in his word. Numbers 23 reminds us that God is not a man that he should lie. I don't know about you, but that gives me a strong feeling of security knowing that I can whole heartedly put my trust in GOD. Do you have a bestfriend? What gave you the confidence to give them that title? Studying and understanding Gods word is what builds our confidence in him. Knowing his character and how he feels about us gives us the confidence we need to go to him boldly with our prayers.

Instead of trying to figure everything out on your own and fight every battle by yourself sometimes it's best to just take a deep breathe and just be still. I know what you're wondering "How can I be still when I'm failing in school? How can I be still when nobody likes me?

How can I be still when I have to take care of my younger siblings because I'm in a single parent household? How can I be still when I'm fighting anxiety daily because I don't fit in?", or whatever else that causes you to stress and worry. Exodus 14:14 is how you can Be Still in the midst of all that you're fighting. If God can make sure that the birds and animals have food to eat, surely because you're way more important, he's going to make sure you have all that you need and the things that you desire. No good thing does the almighty God withhold from us. Everything happens in his impeccable timing, not when we want it to happen because we're not always ready for the things that we are praying for. For instance, if I'm praying to God for a million dollars and I can't manage $100.00 properly, he's not going to bless me with $1,000,000,000 because I would mishandle it. Delayed does not mean denial so don't get discouraged while you wait on the Lord. We learned in week one that God has a plan for our lives and this week you learn that it's his plan that will prevail. If his plan is to give us hope and a future we should have no complaints allowing his plan to lead us in life.
Misunderstood from the hood is what I was for many years of my life. I spent way too many years trying to fit in, instead of stand out like the leader God called me to be. As a young Christians in Christ, I need you to remember that we live in this world, but we are not of this world. The more confident you become in yourself the easier i will be to OWN that truth. Lets catch some vibes from week 2 and digest what we ate this week from the word of God.

Vibes from Week Two

What scripture stood out the most to you this week and why?

Write a List of plans you made for your life without including God.

How will you include him in your plans moving forward?

What did you learn about Gods character?

Meditate on Psalm 84:11 for 24 hours (Reading it multiple times throughout the day) Use this space to jot down how you feel after spending time in Gods word.

LET'S PRAY

DEAR GOD,

THE MORE I GET TO KNOW YOU AND LEARN ABOUT YOU, THE MORE I DESIRE TO WANT TO BE LIKE YOU. HELP ME TO EMBRACE WHAT MAKES ME DIFFERENT AND TO BE REMINDED ALWAYS THAT I LIVE IN THIS WORLD, BUT I'M NOT OF THIS WORLD, THANK YOU FOR BEING A MAN OF YOUR WORD GOD. WHEN THE WORLD AND PEOPLE MAY DISAPPOINT, I CAN ALWAYS PUT MY TRUST IN YOU. AS I CONTINUE TO GROW, I REALLY APPRECIATE YOUR PATIENCE WITH ME. HELP ME TO BE MORE PATIENT WITH MYSELF AS WELL AS OTHERS. WE ALL FIGHT BATTLES, LORD HELP US TO SEEK YOUR HELP INSTEAD OF BEING SCARED TO SURRENDER AS YOUR WORD SAYS WE NEED ONLY TO BE STILL AND YOU WILL FIGHT THE BATTLE FOR US. I KNOW I'M UNDESERVING OF YOUR GOODNESS AND IT MAKES ME LOVE AND APPRECIATE YOU EVEN MORE. HELP MY PLANS ALIGN WITH YOUR PLANS SO THEY HAVE NO CHOICE BUT TO PREVAIL. MY CONFIDENCE IN MYSELF IS GROWING BECAUSE OF THE CONFIDENCE THAT I HAVE IN YOU. YOU'RE WORTHY OF ALL MY PRAISE, AMEN.

THE 10 COMMANDMENTS

EXODUS 20:1-17 KJV

1 And God spake all these words, saying,
2 I am the Lord thy God, which have brought thee out of the land of Egypt, out of the house of bondage.
3 Thou shalt have no other gods before me.
4 Thou shalt not make unto thee any graven image, or any likeness of any thing that is in heaven above, or that is in the earth beneath, or that is in the water under the earth.
5 Thou shalt not bow down thyself to them, nor serve them: for I the Lord thy God am a jealous God, visiting the iniquity of the fathers upon the children unto the third and fourth generation of them that hate me;
6 And shewing mercy unto thousands of them that love me, and keep my commandments.
7 Thou shalt not take the name of the Lord thy God in vain; for the Lord will not hold him guiltless that taketh his name in vain.
8 Remember the sabbath day, to keep it holy.
9 Six days shalt thou labour, and do all thy work:
10 But the seventh day is the sabbath of the Lord thy God: in it thou shalt not do any work, thou, nor thy son, nor thy daughter, thy manservant, nor thy maidservant, nor thy cattle, nor thy stranger that is within thy gates:
11 For in six days the Lord made heaven and earth, the sea, and all that in them is, and rested the seventh day: wherefore the Lord blessed the sabbath day, and hallowed it.
12 Honour thy father and thy mother: that thy days may be long upon the land which the Lord thy God giveth thee.
13 Thou shalt not kill.
14 Thou shalt not commit adultery.
15 Thou shalt not steal.
16 Thou shalt not bear false witness against thy neighbour.
17 Thou shalt not covet thy neighbour's house, thou shalt not covet thy neighbour's wife, nor his manservant, nor his maidservant, nor his ox, nor any thing that is thy neighbour's.

WHAT THE 10 COMMANDMENTS MEAN...

I am the God who saves...

Put God first.

Do not make fake gods.

Do not misuse the name of the Lord your God

Respect God's day of rest.

Respect your parents.

Do not kill people.

Respect marriage promises.

Do not steal.

Do not lie.

Do not be jealous.

Obedience

James 1:25 NIV

But whoever looks intently into the perfect law that gives freedom, and continues in it —not forgetting what they have heard, but doing it—they will be blessed in what they do.

I know you're probably wondering how we jumped from week 2 into the 10 Commandments and the response is simple, we have to obey God. Most people will tell you the goodness of God and talk about the blessings and not share the importance of obedience. Exodus 20:1-17 is the way that God desires for us to live and honestly they are laws that we should want to live by, who wants to be a murderer or a liar? Absolutely no one, that's who.

His laws are to teach us how to be good people, as well as to protect us. Mistakes are inevitable , but its imperative that we try our best daily to be our best. There's a saying, "Once You Know Better, You Do Better" and that's why it's important that you study, understand, and get to know each one. Most of us don't like rules because we want to do things the way we like but can you imagine how chaotic the world would be if we didn't have any rules or laws? God is not the author of chaos and confusion and that's exactly what we would be living in without having to obey. So even in creating the 10 commandments God was show casing his unfailing love for us. Let's get ready for BOLD PRAYERS.

Week 3
BOLD PRAYERS

Ephesians 3:20 NIV
Now to him who is able to do immeasurably more than all we ask or imagine, according to his power that is at work within us

What is your wildest dream? Better yet , if you could plan out the life you desired and that be your reality , what would that look like? Ephesians 3:20 lets us know that God can do more than we can think, ask, or imagine. Did your brain grasp that yet or am I the only one jumping with excitement? God not only has a plan for our lives, but if we trust in him and let him lead us , his plan is going to BLOW OUR MINDS! You may love doing hair and decide that you want to become a beautician, and God's plan is for you to own a salon and help other women become successful stylists. Another example, you love building things and have a dream of working in construction, but God's plan can be for you to start your own construction company. Think Bigger! Believe Bigger! The days of thinking very little for ourselves are over. I don't care how your life has been so far, God wants you to have great expectations because you can trust that he will transform you. When I was a teenager, I made so many mistakes.

Who was Ms. Know It All? Me! From trying alcohol with my friends to lying to my parents to get my way. I've had my fair share of mess ups and I'm not proud of any of it. The reason I'm sharing is so that you can see Gods work first hand through me. He was able help me get back on track and turn my mess into a message and he will do the same for you. You're now qualified to come before the throne of Grace with your BIG, BOLD Prayers! Week three's scriptures are going to help us go to God in confidence, believing we are worthy enough to experience the goodness of God in ways you can't imagine.

What's does your dream life look like in your mind ?

Week 3 Scriptures

Ephesians 3:12 (NIV) - In him and through faith in him we may approach God with freedom and confidence.

Romans 8:31-32 (NIV) - What, then, shall we say in response to these things? If God is for us, who can be against us? He who did not spare his own Son, but gave him up for us all—how will he not also, along with him, graciously give us all things?

Hebrews 4:16 (NIV) - Let us then approach God's throne of grace with confidence, so that we may receive mercy and find grace to help us in our time of need.

Jeremiah 32:27 (NIV) - "I am the Lord, the God of all mankind. Is anything too hard for me?

Matthew 21:21 (NIV) Jesus replied, "What is impossible with man is possible with God."

Luke 18:27 (NIV) - Jesus replied, "Truly I tell you, if you have faith and do not doubt, not only can you do what was done to the fig tree, but also you can say to this mountain, 'Go, throw yourself into the sea,' and it will be done.

John 14:12-14 (NIV) -Very truly I tell you, whoever believes in me will do the works I have been doing, and they will do even greater things than these, because I am going to the Father. 13 And I will do whatever you ask in my name, so that the Father may be glorified in the Son. 14 You may ask me for anything in my name, and I will do it.

I asked you to jot down the life you desired prior to us reading and understanding week three scriptures because I wanted to see if there would be a shift in your thoughts. We just learned that God desires for us to come to him Boldly. Your prayers can move mountains like your fears, your doubts, your worries, your failures, your mistakes, your past, whatever it is that's standing in the way of living the life you desire. Everyone won't understand your journey, and some may even try to talk you out of walking in your purpose, don't let them distract you. If God is for you, it doesn't matter who or what's against you. As children of God, we're not exempt from going through rough times in life, it's knowing we have HIM on our side , leading, guiding, and loving us that's going to keep us going. It's knowing were already Victorious through Christ Jesus that's going to keep us going. It's remembering that God will do exceedingly and abundantly more than we can think, ask, or imagine according to his power that works down on the inside of us that's going to keep us going. He said not only do we possess the power to do what he can, but you can do even greater works but we must first believe. Say it with me , "I Am A BELIEVER"! You're so special to God. He knew this exact moment would be taking place right now, just he knew I would write it.

Let me let you in on a little secret...I didn't know I would write this book either, or the one before it but it was in Gods plan. His good, perfect, and pleasing plan. Your best life is ahead of you , I think you're ready, and God knows you're ready. It's time to put those Big Bold Prayers on paper and watch them come to life!

BIG BOLD PRAYERS

Use the next 3 pages to jot down your BOLD prayers to GOD.

BOLD - showing an ability to take risks; confident and courageous.

BIG BOLD PRAYERS

BOLD - showing an ability to take risks; confident and courageous.

BIG BOLD PRAYERS

BOLD - showing an ability to take risks; confident and courageous.

LET'S PRAY

DEAR GOD,
YOU'RE AWESOME. I'VE GAINED SO MUCH UNDERSTANDING THESE PAST 3 WEEKS THROUGH YOUR WORD. IT'S EXCITING TO KNOW THAT I HAVE A REAL RELATIONSHIP WITH THE CREATOR OF THE HEAVENS AND THE EARTH, THE KING OF KINGS, THE PRINCE OF PEACE! HELP ME TO REMEMBER THAT WHEN OBSTACLES IN LIFE ARISE. KNOWING THAT I CAN BRING ANYTHING BEFORE YOU ,AND YOU WILL BE THERE BECAUSE YOU CARE, GIVES ME SO MUCH HOPE FOR MY PROSPEROUS FUTURE. I AM FORGIVEN, I AM LOVED, I AM QUALIFIED TO DO WHAT YOU'VE CALLED ME TO DO, AND I'M WORTHY TO LIVE THE LIFE I DESIRE ACCORDING TO YOUR WILL. PLEASE COVER MY FAMILY, FRIENDS, AND ALL THE OTHER TEENS WHO ARE EMBARKING ON THIS JOURNEY. HELP US TO TRUST IN YOU AT ALL TIMES. YOU'RE FAITHFUL GOD, AND NOT A MAN THAT YOU SHOULD LIE. BLESS OUR COMMUNITIES, CHURCHES, SCHOOLS, GOVERNMENT, AND NATION. LORD HEAL THE SICK AND BROKEN HEARTED, BRING UNITY IN THE MIDST OF CHAOS AND CONFUSION, PROVIDE FOR THE POOR. ALL THINGS ARE POSSIBLE WITH YOU AND THROUGH YOU. I BRING THESE REQUESTS TO YOU BOLDLY GOD. THANKING YOU GOD IN ADVANCE AND STANDING IN EXPECTATION OF SEEING YOU MOVE IN YOUR PERFECT TIMING. FAVOR IS MY PORTION. ALL PRAISES, GLORY, AND HONOR GOES TO YOU. IN JESUS MIGHTY NAME, AMEN.

Made in the USA
Columbia, SC
10 September 2022

66918806R00017